Taking Action

TAKING ACTI

D1539629

Youth Crime

Jacqui Bailey

rosen publishing's
rosen central

New York

Published in 2010 by The Rosen Publishing Group Inc.
29 East 21st Street, New York, NY 10010

First Edition

Editor: Camilla Lloyd
Consultant: Jayne Wright
Designer: Tim Mayer
Picture researcher: Kathy Lockley

Library of Congress Cataloging-in-Publication Data

Bailey, Jacqui.
  Taking action against youth crime / Jacqui Bailey. – 1st ed.
    p. cm. – (Taking action)
  ISBN 978-1-4358-5346-1 (library binding)
  ISBN 978-1-4358-5476-5 (paperback)
  ISBN 978-1-4358-5477-2 (6-pack)
  1. Juvenile delinquency. 2. Juvenile delinquency–Prevention. I.
Title.
  HV9069.B26 2010
  364.36–dc22

                          2008053526

Picture acknowledgments: The author and publisher would like to thank the
following for allowing their pictures to be reproduced in this publication:
Cover photograph: Neil Geugan/zefa/Corbis. ACE STOCK LIMITED/Alamy:
6B; Bettman/Corbis: 10; Bubbles Photolibrary/Alamy:
13, 43; Chris Collins/Corbis: 33; Christel Gerstenberg/Corbis: 8-9; David
Hoffman Photo Library/Alamy: 27; David R. Frazier Inc/Alamy: 4; Doug
Houghton/Alamy: 40-41; Douglas Fisher/Alamy: 11; f1 online/Alamy:
44T; Gabe Palmer/Corbis: 33-34; Gianni Muratore/Alamy: 36T; Iain
Masterton/Alamy: 23, 44-45; Ian Shaw/Alamy: 14; Janine Wiedel
Photolibrary/Alamy: 12, 38; Jeff Morgan social issues/Alamy: 39; John
Birdsall Social Issues Photo Library: 37; John Giles/PA Archive/PA Photos:
31; John Powell/Photofusion Photo Library: 17; Lachetka/Rex Features:
30B; Martin Ruetschi/Keystone/Corbis: 2-3 (bkg), 4T, 8T, 9R, 12T, 16T,
18-19, 20, 21B, 22T, 26T, 29B, 34T, 37B, 40T, 41R, 43, 45R, 46T, 48; Martyn
Vickery/Alamy: 24T, Mika/zefa/Corbis: 24-25; Neil Geugan/zefa/Corbis:
1, 7; Oote Boe Photography/Alamy: 42; Pawel Libera/Alamy: 28T; Philip
Silverman/Rex Features: 6T (bkg), 15 (bkg), 28B (bkg), 32T, 36B (bkg),
30T (bkg), 32B (bkg); PictureNet/Corbis: 16; Randy Faris/Corbis: 21; Rex
Features: 5; Simon de Trey-White/Photofusion Photo Library: 29; Yoan
Varlat/epa/Corbis: 22.

Sources:
BBC: www.bbc.co.uk
Home Office: www.homeoffice.gov.uk
Home Office Report on Crime in England and Wales
Home Office Report on Youth Justice—The Next Steps
Home Office Statistical Bulletin on Young People and Crime
National Association of Youth Courts: www.youthcourt.net
U.S. Dept. of Justice—Office of Juvenile Justice & Delinquency Prevention
Putting U in the Picture, Mobile Bullying Survey 2005:
www.stoptextbully.com
Trust for the Study of Adolescence: www.studyofadolescence.org.uk
U.S. Dept. of Justice, Bureau of Justice Statistics
Youth Justice Board: www.yjb.gov.uk
Youth Justice Board: Youth Justice Annual Statistics
NSPCC Youth Violence Prevention Centre

Manufactured in China

CONTENTS

Chapter 1

What is crime?

Have you ever had anything stolen from you, such as your bike or cell phone? Or have you ever been bullied or attacked? If you have, then a crime was committed (carried out) and you were the victim of that crime.

Breaking the rules

When someone commits a crime, they are doing something illegal (against the law). Laws are the set of rules that a country uses to protect itself, its people, and their belongings. They help us to understand the difference between right and wrong, and they make sure that people are punished correctly when they break the rules.

A country's government or ruler makes laws. Usually, the laws develop over hundreds of years. Laws can only work properly when people agree to keep them. We all have the right to live our lives without fear of violence or harm, but we also have a responsibility to keep our laws and to support the people who uphold these laws, such as the police.

There are police forces in most countries. The police try to stop people from breaking the law and try to catch those who do.

Many people blamed Sir Paul Condon, who was head of London's Police Force, for the failure of the police to bring Stephen Lawrence's killers to justice.

Crime and punishment

If a crime is committed and the police can collect enough evidence about who was responsible, they can arrest the person and charge them (formally accuse them of the crime). That person may then be sent to a law court to be tried and judged.

If the court decides that an accused person is not guilty, they are set free. If they are found guilty, the judge gives them a suitable sentence. Sentences vary depending on the seriousness of the crime. In Britain, crimes like burglary and murder carry an automatic prison sentence. In some countries, serious crimes such as murder are punishable by death.

In the media

In 1993, Stephen Lawrence, an 18-year-old black school student living in London, was stabbed to death by a group of white youths. The youths did not know Stephen, and it appears that they killed him just because he was black. Although people saw the crime and the police arrested five boys, local people were unwilling to help the police and the boys were released. In 1996, the same youths were put on trial, but the court decided there was not enough evidence against them. Later, a public inquiry blamed the police for not searching more carefully for evidence at the time of the murder. So far, no one has been found guilty of Stephen's murder, although his family still hope that one day the killers will be punished.

Are you old enough?

Young children who commit crimes are not usually put on trial or punished for crimes if they are below the age of criminal responsibility. This is because they are too young to fully realize what they have done. In the U.S.A., the age of criminal responsibility varies—from 6 in N. Carolina to 10 in Wisconsin. Some States do not have a minimum age, but common law states it is 7. In Canada, the age is 12, in Britain it is 10. However, courts can decide that a child involved in crime needs special care.

Once above the age of criminal responsibility, a young person can be arrested and tried, usually in a juvenile court, and their punishment may be different to that of an adult. Young people are still not completely responsible for their lives until they reach the age of majority (usually between 18 and 21). This is the age at which they are considered to be adults and fully responsible for their actions.

Some laws only affect you while you are young. In the U.S.A., you must be over 21 to buy or drink alcohol in public, and in Britain and Australia, it is illegal to buy alcohol under the age of 18. In many Arab countries, however, it is illegal to drink alcohol at any age.

Youth crimes

Most young people do not break the law, or if they do, their crimes are not serious enough to involve the courts. However, people worry that youth crime is increasing. Research shows that we are most likely to get into trouble with the police when we are young—usually between the ages of 14 and 21—but also that we are most likely to be the victims of crime at this age.

Crimes committed by young people are known as youth, or juvenile, crimes. Most of these crimes involve theft, such as shoplifting and mugging, or assaults and fighting, or drug use and underage drinking, or acts of vandalism, such as damage to people's cars or other property.

Young people might vandalize buildings or cars because they are bored or angry, or just to see if they can get away with it. They do not think about how the damage they do affects other people's lives.

TALK ABOUT

✳ Do you think laws help to make our lives more peaceful?

✳ What do you think would happen if there were no laws? Would our lives be better or worse?

✳ What laws would you change if you could, or what extra laws would you have?

For ideas on how to extend Talk About discussions, please see the Notes for Teachers on page 47.

Chapter 2

Crime past and present

The first laws we know of were made more than 4,000 years ago. They dealt with many of the same kinds of crimes we have today. People were punished for harming others or stealing from them, and crimes of murder were punished by death.

Changing times

As our way of life changes, our laws change, too. In the Middle Ages, people believed in magic and feared witches. In Europe, it was a crime to be a witch, and between 1400 and 1700, thousands of adults and children were executed for witchcraft. There are no laws against witchcraft in Europe today.

In Britain, the last execution for witchcraft took place in 1716, although the laws against witchcraft were only finally abolished in 1951. In some parts of Africa and Asia, people are still tried and killed for witchcraft today.

Between the 1700s and 1800s, Britain's towns and cities grew quickly. As they grew, so did the number of poor people living in them. People begged or stole to stay alive and crime increased. Punishments were swift and severe. More than 200 crimes were punishable by hanging, including pickpocketing and stealing food. Some criminals avoided the death penalty by being transported to North America or Australia instead.

By the mid-1800s, people had come to realize how harsh these punishments were. Transportation was ended and the number of crimes punishable by death was reduced. Today, in the U.K., Australia, and in many other countries, the death penalty has been abolished.

Creating crime

Sometimes, new laws create crimes that didn't exist before. In 1920, the U.S. government was worried about people drinking, so it made the manufacture and sale of alcohol illegal. Crime gangs, such as the Mafia, instantly started making and selling illegal alcohol. Between 1920 and 1933, about half-a-million people went to prison before the government admitted that its alcohol laws had created more problems than they had solved. The laws were abolished, but it is still illegal to buy alcohol in some U.S. states to this day.

FACTS

✳ The most famous witchcraft trials in North America were those held in Salem between 1692 and 1693.

✳ Salem was one of a group of villages in New England where young women suddenly began to suffer from fits. The fits were believed to be the result of witchcraft.

✳ More than 150 people were arrested and put on trial.

✳ Twenty-nine people were found guilty and 19 of them were hanged.

✳ One man died while being questioned, and a number of others died while they were in prison.

✳ Three hundred years later, in 2001, all those found guilty at Salem were finally cleared of the charges against them.

Crime stories

Newspapers and magazines love to run exciting stories about daring and clever criminals. We even feel a sneaking admiration for crafty thieves, like the legendary outlaw Robin Hood, who supposedly stole from the rich to give to the poor.

We might think that because some crimes are committed against wealthy businesses, such as banks, rather than against individual people, that no one suffers from them. In reality, someone always suffers and no matter how clever the crimes seem, they are always sadder, more shameful, and less thrilling than the stories about them.

Today, the story of criminals Bonnie and Clyde has become a romantic legend. But in the 1930s, the young couple led a vicious gang of bank robbers who killed at least 13 people. In the end, they were ambushed and gunned down by law officers.

The (Not-So-Great) Train Robbery

One of the most famous crimes in British history is the Great Train Robbery. In 1963, a gang of 15 people highjacked a train traveling to London. The train was carrying money and other valuables from various Scottish banks and other companies, and the gang got away with £2.6 million (worth about $60 million today).

All but two members of the gang were arrested and sent to prison for 30 years, although three of them later escaped and fled the country. One of these, Ronnie Biggs, ended up in South America, where he lived until 2001. At the age of 71, sick and running out of money, he returned to the U.K., where he was sent back to jail to finish his sentence. Over the years, a number of books and movies were produced that turned the robbery into an adventure. But the train driver who was hit over the head at the time was never able to work again, and the robbers themselves spent years locked up in prison.

Scared off

Sometimes stories about violent crimes are frightening and shocking, and can make us feel anxious and unsafe. However, newspapers and television programs do not often include stories about why people commit these crimes, or what is being done to help them to stop offending again. Many of us are left feeling that there is nothing we can do to protect ourselves or to stop the violence, even though we may not have seen or suffered directly from such crimes ourselves.

The headlines we see in the newspapers can make people think that violent crime is getting much worse, even if it isn't.

 TALK ABOUT

Think about how you feel when you read stories about crime.

✱ **Do they make you more worried about crime, or less?**

✱ **Do you think newspapers report crime stories fairly, or do they tend to write about the more shocking or exciting crimes?**

Chapter 3

Why does youth crime happen?

Have you ever committed a crime? In a survey of young people from 10 to 25 years old in England and Wales, 25 percent said they had broken the law in the previous 12 months, although many of these offenses were fairly minor.

Age matters

Age matters when it comes to crime. Boys are much more likely to commit crimes between the ages of 16 and 19, and girls are more likely to do so between the ages of 14 and 15. However, as young people grow older, there is a dramatic drop in the amount of crime they commit.

The reason for this may be that teenagers are easily influenced by each other, especially if they lack a caring family to support them. Also, teenagers can be so involved in their own feelings that they do not always stop to think how their actions might hurt someone else.

Research shows that young people who get involved in activities or interests outside school, such as skateboarding or rollerblading, are less likely to commit crimes.

For the thrill

When young people are not in school or college, they often spend a lot of time hanging out with their friends. If there is nothing for them to do and nowhere interesting for them to go, they may become bored. Committing crimes is one way of making life seem exciting when it isn't—until they get caught!

Alcohol and drugs

People are also more likely to take risks and commit crimes when they are drinking alcohol or taking drugs. Statistics show that about one in three acts of youth vandalism was committed when the offenders were drunk, and people using illegal drugs sometimes steal to get money to buy them. However, not all stealing can be blamed on drug use. It could also be that the type of person willing to risk taking drugs or getting drunk is also the type who is willing to risk carrying out a crime.

Using or selling illegal drugs is a crime in itself, and can lead to committing other types of crime.

It happened to me

"I stole some old lady's handbag once. She was sitting on a seat in the shopping mall and her handbag was on the floor. I just grabbed it and ran. It wasn't for the money. I just did it for fun, and 'cause my friends bet me I wouldn't. Then I started thinking about my grandma, and how she'd feel if someone took her bag. Wish I hadn't done it, now."

Darren, 15.

Rich and poor

Sometimes young people think crime is an easy way to get things they don't have. If they are poor, they may feel angry at those who have more than them. However, not all poor people steal, and poverty is not the only cause of crime.

Hitting back

Young people can also feel frustrated and angry about their lives, and powerless to change things. These feelings might be caused by something small, such as boredom, or by a bigger problem, such as mental illness or abuse. Committing crimes may be their way of getting their own back or lashing out at the world. This might make them feel better for a little while, but it won't help them in the long run.

Many elderly people live in fear of crime, especially if they are on their own. But we should take care of our older people, and remember that one day we will be old, too.

Who suffers?

It may take just seconds or minutes to commit a crime, but its effects can last for much longer. Imagine how you would feel if your home was broken into or your family's possessions were stolen? Would you feel angry? Maybe you would feel frightened, too, and worried that it would happen again? Many victims of crime feel emotionally threatened and insecure, and these feelings can last for a long time. If people have been physically attacked, they may be left permanently injured or in bad health. Sometimes the victims of crime become so nervous or depressed that they are unable to go to work or to school.

Making life difficult

Even crimes aimed at businesses or public spaces have victims. If a company or business is robbed, it may have to close down and people might lose their jobs. Or the company may have to increase its prices to try to replace its losses. This means its customers end up paying for the crime. Damage and destruction of public property, such as buses, trains, phone booths, trees, and public buildings, affects us all. It makes our lives more difficult and it makes the areas we live in ugly and depressing.

TALK ABOUT

* Do you know anyone who has been a victim of crime?
* How do you think they feel about it?
* In what ways do you think crime affects your neighborhood?
* Why do you think those crimes happen?

Chapter 4

Behaving badly

Behaving badly doesn't sound very serious, does it? To some people, behaving badly is the same thing as having a good time or getting drunk. However, bad behavior is one of the biggest causes of social problems and unhappiness. Behaving badly might mean being noisy in public places, or smashing windows, dumping litter, or spraying graffiti.

Are you antisocial?

Bad behavior is known as antisocial behavior, or sometimes juvenile delinquency. It is mainly seen as a youth problem, although adults behave badly, too. Some types of antisocial behavior, for instance, trashing a car, are criminal, and laws exist to deal with them. In other cases, such as shoplifting, it might be up to the victim to decide whether or not they want to take an offender to court.

One common form of antisocial behavior is painting graffiti on other people's property. Some people think that graffiti is an art form and should be allowed, but many others are upset by it and feel that it damages their property or spoils their surroundings.

TALK ABOUT

Which of the following reasons do you think might make someone more likely to behave in an antisocial way?

✱ They or their friends or other members of their family have been in trouble with the police before.

✱ They drink a lot of alcohol or take drugs.

✱ Their parents do not care about their behavior.

✱ There is a lot of antisocial behavior where they live.

✱ There is nothing for young people to do in their area.

Repairing the damage

Many antisocial acts are not serious enough to justify an arrest and trial, even though they may frighten people. Instead, the police and other authorities aim to deal with these acts in a way that will punish the offender and help them not to offend again.

In the United States, young offenders might attend a "juvenile court," or "teen court," where they are tried and judged by adults and people their own age. In the U.K., they may be given a formal warning by the police and asked to sign an Acceptable Behavior Contract (ABC) agreeing to change and improve their behavior.

The kind of sentence the offender is likely to get could include having to apologize to the victim and pay for any damage to be repaired. They might have to do some kind of unpaid community work. They may also have to attend a learning program to help them understand the reasons for their behavior.

Many adults think antisocial behavior by young people is worse than it actually is. Sometimes this is because of the way young people dress. Wearing hooded sweatshirts or "hoodies," for example, can make older people think that the wearer is deliberately hiding his or her face in order to do something wrong without being recognized.

Bullying

Bullying is one type of antisocial behavior that can happen anywhere—at school, at work, or in the home. Bullying includes teasing someone, leaving them out, making rude remarks, spreading hurtful rumors about them, stealing or damaging their property, physically threatening or hurting them, or forcing them to do things they don't want to do.

Up to one in three children and young people experience some kind of bullying, although most never report it to an adult. In the past, bullying was thought to be just part of growing up. Now, we know that it is harmful and should be taken seriously. It causes great hurt and unhappiness, often much more than even the bullies themselves might mean at the time.

The damage it does

Being bullied can make young people anxious and afraid, and damage their self-confidence. Some victims of bullying become so depressed that they harm themselves, or even commit suicide. Or they might lash out at others as a way of getting their own back, or even become bullies themselves.

FACTS

* **Boys are more likely to be bullied, or to bully others, than girls.**
* **Bullying happens more often among young teens than older teens.**
* **Children who are badly treated or neglected at home are more likely to be bullied or excluded (left out) at school. They are also more likely to be bullies.**
* **Research carried out in the United States has found that bullies are four times more likely to commit crimes as they get older than nonbullies.**

What to do

Bullying is always wrong and it can be stopped.
No one should ever have to put up with being bullied.
It is also important that the bullies themselves are
helped to realize what they are doing and to change.

If you are being bullied, or you know someone who is,
it is important that you tell an adult you can trust. Most
bullying happens around schools and colleges, but it
can also happen at home. Children may be bullied by
their parents, guardians, or other family members, but
some teenagers bully their parents, too. Bullying at
home is sometimes called child abuse or domestic
violence (see page 28). Schools have their own powers
for dealing with bullying, but if it includes assault
(being physically attacked), theft, or racism, then the
police may get involved

*If bullies are allowed to get
away with frightening and
attacking people, they are
more likely to go on to
commit other crimes as
they get older.*

Cybercrime

Crimes carried out on computers, the Internet, or involving telephones are known as cybercrimes. One of the most common forms of cybercrime is cyberbullying. Receiving rude or threatening text messages or phone calls may make you angry, but it can also leave you feeling helpless and scared.

Some cyberbullies use cameras on their cell phones to send embarrassing or violent photos of others, taken without their permission. In the U.K., a very nasty type of cyberbullying is known as "happy slapping," in which gangs attack innocent people and film the attack on their phones.

These videos are then put on Internet sites or sent to other people. The reason gangs do this is to make themselves look good, but happy slapping is vicious and cowardly. It is also a serious crime, which can lead to a prison sentence.

Images of so-called "happy slapping" are, in fact, a record of violent bullying. How would you feel if this happened to you?

Network nasties

The Internet is a great way to stay in touch, but the downside is that some people use it to send spiteful emails, or to set up a website about someone and then invite others to put horrible remarks on it.

Chatrooms make it easy for people to tell lies about themselves. You could find that the friendly 13-year-old girl you think you have been talking to online is really a creepy 35-year-old man. Some adults who abuse young people are known to use the Internet to find their victims. It is unsafe to plan to meet an online friend over the Internet, no matter how great they may seem, especially if they want to meet in secret.

Cybersafety

If you are the victim of cyberbullying, make sure you tell your parents or another responsible adult so they can report it to the police and to your Internet service provider. Cyberbullies often think they can hide their identity, but the police can trace abusive calls, texts, emails, and websites back to the original phone or computer.

It is never safe to give out personal information about yourself on the Internet, or to put lots of pictures of yourself on your website, even if you think your site is protected.

DOs & DON'Ts

✱ **Always report cyberbullying to your school or college, or to the police.**

✱ **Do look at the Internet for advice on how to deal with cyberbullying. See page 47 for some useful websites.**

✱ **If you receive any nasty text messages or phone calls, get a new SIM card for your cell phone.**

✱ **Never give anyone your full name, address, or phone number on the Internet.**

✱ **Don't reply to abusive phone calls or other messages, but keep them as evidence and tell your parents or an adult you trust.**

✱ **Don't give your phone number to people you don't know or trust. Ask your friends not to pass on your number to others without asking you first.**

Chapter 5

Crimes of theft

Theft means taking something from someone without his or her permission and without intending to give it back. More people commit theft than any other type of crime. Having something stolen makes a person feel miserable and angry.

Pickpockets and shoplifters

There are lots of different types of theft. Pickpockets, for example, steal things from someone's purse or pocket without the person noticing. Pickpocketing takes some skill, but this does not stop children, as well as adults, from becoming pickpockets.

Shoplifting takes little skill. Shoplifting is the theft of goods from a store by someone who is pretending to be a customer. Young people often shoplift to find out what it feels like, or as a dare. Usually, they only do it once or twice.

Pickpockets like to work in crowded places, such as busy streets, on buses, trains, or at public events, where people are distracted by the things going on around them.

For the buzz

However, for some people shoplifting becomes a habit. This may be because they do not have the money to buy things, or because it gives them a buzz and makes them feel better about their lives, for a while at least.

Because stores suffer such big losses from shoplifting, they will almost always hand offenders over to the police. Shoplifting is unfair on the rest of us, because we end up paying more for our goods to cover the cost of those that are stolen.

Piracy

Theft isn't only about taking a physical object. Downloading a piece of software from the Internet without paying for it, such as a computer game or a song, is software piracy, and it is a crime. It is stealing someone else's copyright, especially if the software is copied onto a CD or DVD and then sold. Copyright is the legal ownership of a creative work. Writers, musicians, and filmmakers make their living from the copyrights they own, so if other people steal their copyright, it is the same as stealing their salary.

The making and selling of pirate DVDs is a big business. Pirates can make thousands or even millions of pounds, and often use the money to pay for other crimes, such as smuggling drugs or guns.

It happened to me

"I was doing a vacation job at Christmas time to get some money to buy presents and stuff. I'd just been paid and had a lot of cash in my purse. On the bus, I got my purse out to pay my bus fare and then put it back in my handbag. When I got off the bus, a man got off right behind me and bumped into me a little. When I got home, my purse wasn't in my bag any longer and all my money was gone. I know he took it and he was, like, a grown up and he didn't look poor or anything."

Rachael, 16.

If you are offered cheap jewelry, CDs, or DVDs, electronic equipment or designer-label clothes, you may be buying stolen goods and encouraging others to commit burglary.

"I've been robbed!"

When a thief uses force to steal, it is called robbery. If a person is robbed in a public place, it is known as mugging. There has been a steady increase in mugging since the 1970s, when people began carrying personal electronics and other expensive equipment around with them. In the past ten years, however, figures for street crime have fallen for some of us, but for young people from 12 to 19 years old, the figures have risen.

The reason for this rise appears to be that more young people are likely to be out on the streets in the evening, and to be carrying cell phones or MP3 players. Often, the muggers are also young people. The muggers may be a group of older boys threatening a younger boy to hand over his phone, or muggings may be more serious crimes involving violence, and sometimes, even murder.

Mugging is always a frightening crime, so it is important to be aware of your personal safety. Try to avoid traveling on your own at night and stay away from quiet, badly-lit places. Keep your personal possessions out of sight. If muggers stop you, it is safest to hand over whatever you have without arguing with them, even if it makes you angry. Make sure you report the mugging to the police.

TALK ABOUT

* Do you think anyone ever has the right to steal something from someone else?

* Do you think it makes any difference if the person being stolen from is rich?

* How do you think you would feel if someone stole something from you or your family?

Break in

If someone breaks into a building or a vehicle in order to commit a crime, it is called burglary, or breaking and entering. Climbing into a property through an open window is called trespassing. And doing so with the intention of committing a crime is still burglary.

Burglary is a serious crime. Offenders are usually sent to prison or a youth offender institution. If the burglars are carrying weapons, even if they do not use them, it is known as "aggravated burglary" and could be punishable by life imprisonment.

Burglars often wreck the property they break into, whether they steal anything or not. Aside from the loss and damage to their property, victims are left feeling shock, fear, anger, and depression, which can affect them for a long time.

Chapter 6

Crimes of violence

Violent crimes are the worst crimes and most of us fear them, especially when there are so many news stories about them. In fact, violent crimes happen less often than we think. Throughout the world, only about 10 percent to 15 percent of all reported crimes are violent crimes, and in countries such as the United States and the U.K., violent crimes are decreasing.

What are violent crimes?

A violent crime is when force, or threat of force, is used against another person. It may be a minor assault, such as pushing someone, or the most serious crime of all—murder. In law, murder means deliberately causing another person's death.

Accidentally causing someone's death, by drunken or careless driving, for example, is usually called manslaughter and is a slightly less serious crime. Other violent crimes include robbery and sexual offenses such as rape.

FACTS

Crime figures in England and Wales in 2006–7 show that:

✳ About half of the violent crimes reported to the police did not actually involve physical injury to the victim.

✳ The risk of being a victim of any type of violent crime was 3.6% (roughly one person in every 28).

✳ Young men between the ages of 16 and 24 were most at risk of being a victim of some kind of violent crime.

✳ Around two-thirds of the violent events reported to the police were carried out by people known to the victim.

Why do they happen?

Most violent crimes are fairly minor acts of aggressive behavior—people attacking or threatening others because they are bigger or stronger, or because they are greater in number. Violent crimes often occur alongside other crimes, such as theft and mugging, or because the offender is drunk or on drugs.

Some people admire others who behave in violent ways. They may see violence on television, or in movies and computer games, and think it is acceptable to use violence to get what you want. Among street gangs, fighting and violence is often seen as a way of proving yourself and gaining respect from others. Offenders do not think about the misery they cause to their victims and to their victims' families.

Often, violent acts lead to more violence, either in anger or revenge, or because minor crimes of street violence can easily lead to bigger, more serious crimes. Organized crime gangs threaten or assault people as part of their business, and to make sure that everyone is so frightened of them that no one will tell the police what they are up to.

Learning about the dangers of violent behavior can help prevent children from joining street gangs.

27

Domestic violence

Violent crimes do not only happen between strangers or on the street. Domestic violence means any kind of threat, attack, or abuse carried out between people who are living together or who have lived together. Although most domestic violence is carried out by men against women, there are instances of women carrying it out. It can also be adult violence against children, or children behaving violently toward one another, or older children behaving violently toward their parents.

Domestic violence is a type of bullying. You do not have to be physically hit or injured to suffer from domestic violence, it can also count as violence if you are forced to do things against your will, or are not allowed to live a normal life, such as seeing your friends, getting a job, or handling your own money. Because domestic violence happens at home, it is often kept secret and victims can feel that it is somehow their fault. Domestic violence is never the fault of the victim. It is a crime and it can be stopped.

Domestic violence can happen in any family, regardless of race, religion, background, or how much money you have.

Sexual assault

If you are bullied, talked to, or touched in a way that makes you feel uncomfortable, you may have been assaulted. If someone makes you have sex with them against your will it is called rape. Rape and sexual assault are crimes of violence.

The important thing to remember is that no matter who the offender is, or how it happened, it is never the victim's fault. It is vital for them to get help, both for themselves and to stop the offender from doing it again.

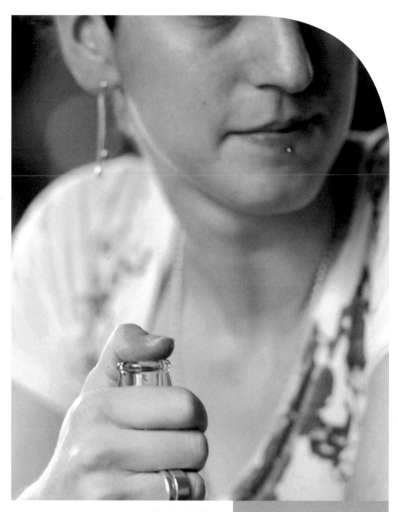

Young people are particularly at risk from sexual assault as a result of drinking too much or taking drugs. Date-rape drugs are colorless and tasteless, and may be put into a person's drink while they are not watching. The drugged victim becomes confused and unable to take care of themselves. They may not even realize they have been raped until some days later.

DOs & DON'Ts

If you, or someone you know, is a victim of domestic violence:

✳ Tell an adult you can trust about what is happening.

✳ Get advice from a helpline or website, such as Childhelp (see page 47 for some suggestions).

✳ Try to talk to the victim and encourage them to get help.

✳ If adults are fighting, don't try to stop them or you may get hurt, too. Instead call the police emergency number.

Street violence

According to statistics, teenagers and young adults between the ages of 12 and 24 are most at risk from violent crime. Those between 14 and 19 years old are particularly at risk. However, it is worth remembering that many of the crimes that are counted as violent crimes involve little or no physical injury, even though they may include the threat of injury.

Much of the violence that happens between young people has to do with street crimes, such as bullying, fighting, mugging, and other thefts. The use of alcohol and drugs fuel the violence. People who are drunk or "high" are often aggressive, and an argument between two people can easily worsen into a fight involving friends and strangers.

Also, as with happy slapping (see page 20), there seems to be a fascination with filming street fights and posting them on Internet websites. Some people think this peculiar interest in fighting has grown out of the popularity of violent video fight games, but it may have more to do with the spread of the Internet and the addition of video cameras to cell phones.

Soccer fans are well-known for attacking one another after or even during major games, especially if they have been drinking. But they aren't the only ones. Baseball, basketball, and ice hockey fans may also fight for their team.

Sometimes people are attacked or threatened just because they belong to a different race, color, or religion, or are different in some other way. These actions are known as hate crimes. Hate crimes cause enormous suffering and destroy people's peace and ability to live their lives freely.

In the media

Ten-year-old Damilola Taylor was on his way home one afternoon in November 2000, when he was stopped by a group of boys who lived on the same housing project in south London. The boys were a few years older than Damilola and they belonged to a local gang. They began bullying Damilola and one boy stabbed him in the leg with a broken bottle. Damilola staggered to a doorway, where he was found bleeding to death. The stabbing had been meant to frighten Damilola into doing what the gang wanted, but instead, the glass had cut an artery and Damilola died on the way to hospital.

Gang violence

Street gangs often fight each other over their territory. They also use violence to punish members of other gangs who they believe have insulted or harmed them in some way. Gang members place a lot of importance on appearing tough and fearless.

Street gangs exist in almost every major city in the world, mainly in areas where there is poverty and unemployment. Being part of a gang gives young people, particularly boys, a sense of purpose and belonging, and some protection from other gangs. It also gives them a way of making money, usually through theft, or buying and selling drugs.

Belonging to a street gang can seem exciting, or even necessary if everyone you know is in a gang. However, the harsh truth is that gang members often end up hurt, hooked on drugs, in prison, or dead. Although gang life may be difficult to avoid, especially if you are already a member, it is important to think about it carefully, and ask yourself if this is really what you want to do with your life.

Carrying weapons

A weapon is anything that can be used to attack or hurt someone. It may be a gun, a knife, a brick, or even a piece of broken glass. In most countries, there are laws against people carrying weapons in public, particularly guns and knives. These laws apply even if people do not use the weapons.

In the U.K., for example, it is against the law for anyone to carry a sharp or long-bladed knife in public, or to sell a knife to anyone under the age of 16. People who own guns must have a license to carry and use them, and keep them locked up when they are not in use. Unfortunately, this does not stop some criminals from buying and using guns illegally.

On the street

The number of gun crimes is very low in the U.K.—less than half of 1 percent of all recorded crimes. Most illegal guns are used by organized crime gangs involved in drug dealing or major robberies. However, recently there has been a rise in gun and knife crimes among young people, especially among street gangs.

Knives are mainly carried by boys and young men. They think these weapons will give them a tougher reputation, or will protect them against other people with weapons. There are more people carrying guns, too. These may be real guns, or fakes ("replicas"). Guns are often carried just to impress others, but owning and carrying them is only a step away from using them. A number of teenagers and young children have been injured or killed by knives and guns, sometimes deliberately but also by accident.

Carrying imitation, or replica guns is against the law and may be as dangerous as carrying the real thing. From a distance, it can be hard for the police or anyone else to tell the difference, and the owner of the replica could end up being killed by the real thing.

Terrorists

The other criminals who use weapons are terrorists. A terrorist is someone who threatens violence or carries out acts of violence for political reasons, for example, to weaken a country's government or beliefs. Young people who are unhappy or discontented with their own lives are sometimes recruited by terrorists to carry out political activities and acts of violence.

One of the worst acts of terrorism in recent years was when terrorist highjackers captured four passenger airliners, and forced two of them to fly into the World Trade Center buildings in New York. Thousands of ordinary people were killed.

TALK ABOUT

* Do you think carrying knives and guns makes people more or less violent?
* How do you think the way that guns and knives are used in adventure movies and computer games affects the way we think about them?

Chapter 7

What happens if you commit a crime?

One minute you are just spending time with your friends, the next you are being questioned by the police or, even worse, being taken to the police station.

Stop and search

The police are there to prevent crimes, protect our safety and to find the people who commit crimes. To help them do this, they are allowed to stop anyone in the street or in a car and ask them questions. They may also ask you to empty your pockets or open your bags so they can search them for drugs, stolen property, or weapons.

It happened to me

"Last year, my brother got caught smashing a store window. My dad went to the police station. He paid for the window to be repaired, and my brother had to sign this agreement with the police saying that he would come home straight from school and not hang out with his friends. He had to be home by six every evening and couldn't go out for three months. Not that he had any money to go out, anyway, 'cause Dad stopped his pocket money. He was really fed up, but Dad said it was his own fault for being so stupid, and he knew it was, too."

John, 12.

Getting told off

If it is the first time you have been in trouble (a first offense), the police can decide not to formally charge you. If the crime is not serious and you admit that you did it, they may give you a reprimand instead. A reprimand is an official warning, or "telling off." It takes place at a police station, and if you are 17 or under, your parent or guardian may have to be there. There may also be someone from the juvenile justice system, who will make sure that your case is dealt with properly.

Changing your ways

As well as being given a reprimand, you could be given a court probation order that limits the places you can go or the people you can see. You might also have to perform tasks such as community work or attend special classes. Failing to obey is a criminal offense, for which you can be arrested and taken to court.

In Britain, these orders are called Antisocial Behavior Orders (ASBOs). British juveniles may also be asked to sign a contract agreeing to change their behavior, known as an Acceptable Behavior Contract.

If you get into trouble again, or if your offense is more serious, you may be formally charged with committing a crime and you will have to appear in court. This also applies if you refuse to agree with the police that you have done anything wrong (in other words, if you say you are "not guilty").

The police do not only stop people when they are suspicious of them, they may also stop you to ask if you have seen anything or if you know someone they are looking for.

A fair trial

Anyone accused of a crime has the right to a fair trial. The case against them must be heard by a judge who is not prejudiced in any way. Witnesses are allowed to give evidence for or against the accused person without being threatened or made to change their story, and the accused person is defended by a lawyer.

In the U.S.A., if you are over the age of criminal responsibility for your state, and are accused of a crime, your case will be dealt with by the juvenile justice system and usually heard in a juvenile court. If it is a serious crime, the juvenile court may pass your case on to an adult court.

If it is thought necessary, offenders may have to wear an electronic personal identity device, or "tag," to make sure that they keep to the rules set by their bail, or by their sentence.

On bail

When you have been charged, you can usually go home to wait for your trial. This is known as being let out "on bail." Your bail might have certain rules attached to it, such as having to be at home or at school at certain times each day (a curfew), or having to report to the police station at regular times. If the police think you might get into more trouble or might be at risk of harming yourself or others, you might have to stay in a special residential facility while you wait for your trial.

Most countries have special courts for young people. Generally the judges and other court officials are used to dealing with young offenders and their families. Their aim is to help offenders correct their behavior, as well as come up with a suitable punishment.

FACTS

* The total number of offenses committed in England and Wales by young people from 10 to 17 years old in the year 2005–6, was 301,860 (from a total population of 10 to 17 year olds of almost 5.5 million).

* More than 80% of the offenses were committed by boys.

* Over 85% of the offenders were white, 5.8% were black, 3.1% were Asian, and the rest were of mixed or other races.

* About 45% of the offenses were dealt with out of court, by reprimands and warnings.

* The majority of the offenses were for theft and handling stolen goods (18.5%), violence (18.1%), motoring offenses (15.6%), criminal damage (12.9%), and upsetting public order (7.5%).

(Figures from the *Youth Justice Board Annual Statistics* 2005–6.)

At court

Juvenile courts are smaller and less overpowering than adult courts and the general public is not allowed in. In Britain, three judges usually judge each case. If you are under 16, your parents or guardians must be there. You will also have a lawyer, who will talk to the judges on your behalf.

Your charge is read and you will be asked whether you plead guilty or not guilty. If you plead guilty, the judges will decide what your sentence (punishment) will be. If you plead not guilty, they will listen to the police evidence against you, and your explanation of why you are not guilty. If there are witnesses, the judges will also listen to their descriptions of what happened.

Guilty or not guilty

The judges then decide whether you are guilty or not guilty. If they find you not guilty, you are immediately released from court. If you are guilty, you will be given a sentence. Sometimes the judges say they want a report first, giving them more information about you.

In the community

Depending on the seriousness of the case and how many times you have been in trouble before, you are most likely to have to pay a fine or compensation to the victim, and you will get a sentence in the community. This means you are ordered to do certain things for a period of time, usually from three months to one year, and are supervised (checked) to make sure that you do them.

You may have to go to a training center at weekends, or a treatment center that helps people with alcohol or drug problems. You may have to apologize to your victim, either in person or by letter, and do a certain number of hours each week of unpaid work to make amends to either the victim or the community. For example, you may have to pick up trash from a public park, or help to paint an elderly person's home.

You or your parents may also have to pay some of the costs of holding your trial. If you do not carry out any of the terms of your community sentence, you will be sent back to court and will be given a tougher sentence. You might even be put into custody (see opposite).

Young offenders might have to clean up graffiti as part of their community service.

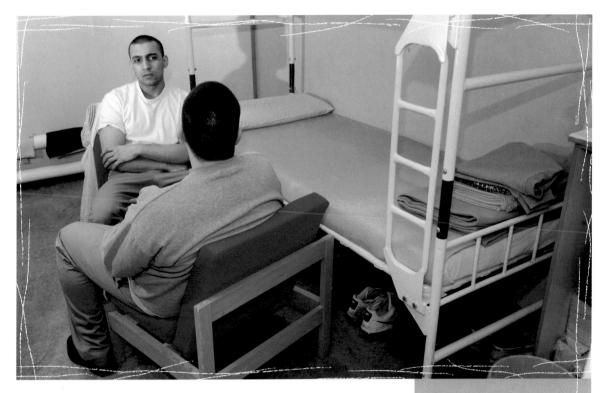

On the inside

If your crime is serious enough, or if you have committed a number of crimes, you could be put in custody. This means that half or two-thirds of your sentence will be spent living in a juvenile residential facility, secure children's home, or a training center.

Juvenile residential facilities try to educate and train offenders so that they will not break the law again, but they are also tough places with strict rules. Custodial sentences can last for a few months or a few years. Very violent crimes can have much longer sentences.

Offenders are not allowed to leave the institution or center except under supervision. They have to go to classes and training sessions to improve their behavior and help with their education or work skills.

TALK ABOUT

✳ **What do you think is the best way to deal with young offenders?**

✳ **Do you think they should be put in prison, or made to work for the local community?**

✳ **How would you feel if the offender was your brother or sister?**

✳ **How would you feel if you were the victim?**

Chapter 8

What can you do about crime?

Crime affects us all. It affects how we feel about ourselves and about our neighbors, our communities, and the different people who control and manage our country and our laws. The police and the court officials deal with crime when it happens, but we all have a responsibility to do whatever we can to stop it happening—both for our own sake and for everyone around us.

Think about it

No one wants to be a victim of crime. Protecting yourself from crime doesn't mean learning to be a martial arts expert or carrying weapons, or even joining a gang to frighten off others. These things are just as likely to lead to trouble as prevent it.

The best way to prevent crime is to stay away from situations where crimes can happen. This means behaving sensibly, thinking about how your actions might affect others, and not taking risks. Before you groan about how boring all that sounds, let's look a little more closely at what this might mean.

Looking after your stuff

Young people are more likely to get their cell phones stolen than anyone else. So if you were given the latest model for your birthday and wanted to show it to your friends, would you wave it around on the street or in the bus?

If you did this, do you think others, as well as your friends, might notice your new phone, too? Might one or more of those people, especially if they were older than you, think that they would like a new phone as well, and try to steal it? If you had kept your phone in your pocket and waited until you were somewhere safer and less public to show it off, do you think you would be less likely to have it stolen?

Taking care of your stuff by not flashing it around or making it easy for someone to steal makes it harder for others to commit crime and helps you keep hold of your belongings.

Always lock up your bike if you have to leave it somewhere in public. If they are easy to remove, take a wheel or the seat with you. Keep a photograph of your bike and mark it in some way to make it recognizable. If it is stolen, report the theft to the police.

DOs & DON'Ts

* **Hide the headphone wires of your MP3 player under your jacket or T-shirt and keep the player in an inside pocket.**

* **Keep your bag under the table by your feet. Never put your bag on the back of a chair or on top of a table.**

* **If you have a bank card, don't carry a note of your PIN number around with it.**

* **Tear up old receipts so that no one can see your card number. Tell the bank right away if your card is lost, even if you are not sure it has been stolen.**

* **Don't put money, wallets, or cell phones in your back pocket, making it easier for a pickpocket to steal them.**

* **Don't wave your money or wallet around where people can see them.**

Looking after yourself

When you are out, pay attention to what is going on around you. You are more likely to be mugged or pickpocketed if you are distracted. Try to avoid gangs or groups of other children, especially if they are just hanging around looking bored.

In the evening, try to travel home with friends. Don't let your friends travel alone, either. If one of them lives far away, ask if they can stay overnight with you—that way, you both have someone to travel with. Keep to roads that are brightly-lit and busy, and don't take shortcuts through alleyways or parks, even if you usually walk through them in the daytime.

If you have to catch a bus on your own at night, choose a stop that is well-lit and has other people waiting at it, even if it is not your nearest one. When you get on the bus, sit near to the driver and choose a seat by the aisle so you can get out easily if you want to.

Don't risk it

Be especially careful if you or your friends are drinking or taking drugs. More accidents, fights, and crimes happen when people are drunk or high on drugs than at other times. Never get into a car with a driver who has been drinking or taking drugs. It is just not worth the risk, no matter how confident they are—that's just the alcohol or the drugs talking. Even if they make fun of you, or you have to get a bus or call your parents for a ride, it is much better to be safe than hurt or killed in a car crash.

Making choices

You may not realize it, but how you behave and the choices you make affect other people as well as yourself. If you commit a crime, you make someone else a victim of crime.
This is also true if you encourage or help another person to commit a crime. Be smart and aim to set a good example, and when you and your friends get bored, try to talk them out of doing things that will get them into trouble.

Being drunk or high on drugs can make people careless and overconfident, or angry and aggressive— all of which mean that we are more likely to do things we wouldn't normally do.

FACTS

* According to research carried out in the United States, young people who regularly drink too much alcohol while they are still growing could be causing long-term damage to their bodies and their brains.

* Binge drinking among young people in the U.K. is on the increase. Children under 16 are now drinking twice as much as they were ten years ago.

* Around half of all violent crimes and almost a third of accidents take place when people are drunk.

Reporting crime

You might think that a victim of a crime, or someone who saw a crime happen, would be so angry and upset that the first thing they would do would be to tell the police. Surprisingly, this is not always what happens.

This might be because the victim thinks the crime is not serious enough and the police won't be interested. Or they might think the police won't be able to do anything, so there is no point telling them. If the crime involved abuse, the victim may feel ashamed about what has happened to them. They might think they had done something that allowed the crime to happen, or that they should have been better at defending themselves.

Sometimes people are afraid to go to the police. They worry they won't be believed or that the police may think they were involved in some way, or that the criminal may harm them or their family.

Need to know

No matter what the crime is, if it is not reported, it means we are allowing criminals to think they can get away with their behavior so they can carry on and commit more crimes. Talking about it also helps you to recover from the shock. With serious crimes, police forces use specially trained people to help the victim to describe their experience and come to terms with their feelings about it. The police will also protect you if they think you are in danger.

Local neighborhood watch schemes like this one in Canada are found all around the world. They encourage everyone to be more involved in looking out for crimes and taking care of their neighbors.

These are a group of neighborhood watch members from Beijing, China.

Even if the crime is not serious, the police need to know about it. Reporting crimes helps them to know what is going on in their area, and to find out who may be involved. If they cannot solve the crime, the information you give them may help them to solve other crimes in the future.

Get involved

Many communities, schools, and colleges, run their own neighborhood watch schemes. Neighborhood watch is an active way for people to get together to make their community safer. By working with the police and other local authorities, neighborhood watch schemes try to make sure that everyone in the neighborhood knows about the crime in their area and is on the lookout for ways to prevent it.

DOs & DON'Ts

* If you have been attacked, or you think a crime may be happening or someone may be in danger, you should dial the emergency service as quickly as possible. Every country has its own 24-hour emergency number, and calls are free. In the United States it is 911, in the U.K. it is 999, in Australia it is 000, and in New Zealand it is 111.

* Don't panic. Try to tell the emergency operator what is happening as quickly and clearly as possible. Make sure you explain where you are and don't hang up until the operator tells you to.

* Don't call the emergency services if it is not a real emergency. If something has been stolen or damaged but no one has been hurt, or if you want to report a crime that has already happened, call or go to your local police station.

* Always report a crime. If you are nervous about going to the police, you can tell Crime Stoppers instead—either by phone, text message, or via the Internet (see page 47).

Glossary

abuse To treat someone in a cruel or violent way, either mentally or physically.

Acceptable Behavior Contract (ABC) In the U.K., a voluntary written agreement between someone who is behaving in an antisocial way and the police, local authority, school, or other people concerned.

arrest To take someone to a police station and keep them there until they have been charged with a crime.

binge drinking Drinking a lot of alcohol (more than six or eight units) in a short space of time, with the main aim of getting drunk.

charged To be officially accused of a crime.

compensation A sum of money paid to someone to make up for the damage or loss they have suffered.

court-ordered probation An official court order that bans or forbids someone from behaving in a certain way, or going to particular places, or seeing particular people. If the order is broken in any way, the offender can be sent back to court to face more serious punishment. In the U.K., this is called an Antisocial Behavior Order (ASBO).

evidence The factual information that proves that a crime has been committed and who has committtted it.

execute To carry out a legal sentence of death.

fine An amount of money you are ordered to pay to a court as a punishment for breaking the law. You can be sent to prison for failing to pay a fine.

license A written document from the police or another authority that gives someone legal permission to do something.

Mafia A secret society led by powerful criminal families, which started in Sicily in the mid-1800s. It then spread to other parts of Italy and to the United States and Australia.

organized crime gangs Criminal organizations, such as the Mafia, that set up illegal businesses to make money out of activities such as drugs, gambling, or threatening legal businesses with damage unless they pay for "protection."

prejudiced Having a bad opinion or dislike of someone without any specific reason.

rape When someone is forced to have sex with another person against their will.

sentence The punishment given to someone for breaking the law.

transported Taken by boat to live and work in a foreign country. From the 1600s to 1850s, Britain sent many of its convicted criminals to work in new settlements in North America and Australia.

tried To be taken before a court and put on trial—investigated and judged—for a crime.

vandalism Deliberately damaging or destroying someone else's property.

Further information and Web Sites

Notes for Teachers:

The Talk About panels are to be used to encourage debate and avoid the polarization of views. One way of doing this is to use "continuum lines." Think of a number of opinions or statements about the topics that can be considered by pupils. An imaginary line is constructed, which pupils can stand along to show what they feel in response to each statement (please see above). If they strongly agree or disagree with the viewpoint, they can stand by the signs; if the response is somewhere in between, they stand along the line in the relevant place. If the response is "neither agree, nor disagree" or they "don't know," then they stand at an equal distance from each sign, in the middle. Continuum lines can also be drawn on paper and pupils can mark a cross on the line to reflect their views.

Books to read

Introducing Issues With Opposing Viewpoints: Crime
Laurie S Friedman
(Greenhaven Press, 2008)

Opposing Viewpoints: Crime and Criminals
James D Torr
(Greenhaven Press, 2004)

What Are My Rights? 95 Questions and Answers About Teens and the Law
Thomas A Jacobs
(Free Spirit Publishing, 1997)

Web Sites

Due to the changing nature of Internet links, Rosen Publishing has developed an online list of Web sites related to the subject of this book. This site is regularly updated. Please use this link to access this list:
http://www.rosenlinks.com/act/yout

Index

Entries in **bold** are for pictures.